The Ultimate Predators In The Wild

Speedy Publishing LLC
40 E. Main St. #1156
Newark, DE 19711

www.speedypublishing.com

Copyright 2014
9781635011098
First Printed October 27, 2014

All Rights reserved. No part of this book may be reproduced or used in any way or form or by any means whether electronic or mechanical, this means that you cannot record or photocopy any material ideas or tips that are provided in this book.

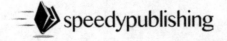

Predator Facts...

Cheetahs are the most amazing animals. Built for high speed, Cheetahs are the experts when it comes to hunting fast, agile prey in broad daylight. Capable of reaching zero to one hundred km/h in seconds, these cats have evolved to develop a sleek and slim body that helps in their highly specialized lifestyle.

Predator Facts...

The most fearsome animal in all Africa may well be the black mamba, the giant venomous snake found throughout the southeastern portion of the continent. It gets its name from the black skin on the inside of its mouth, which it displays just before it strikes. These animals are usually quite shy, but can be extremely aggressive when confronted.

Predator Facts...

Notorious for their sharp teeth and voracious appetites, piranhas inhabit several of the major river basins in South America. These omnivorous fish are known for their taste for meat, although attacks on human beings are quite rare, despite breathless accounts from early explorers.

Predator Facts...

The grizzly bear, also known as the brown bear, is probably the most feared animal in North America. This powerful predatory animal can stand 7 feet tall and weigh more than 800 pounds. Its strong limbs and huge paws can kill a man in a single swipe, and its powerful crushing jaws allow it to feed on a variety of foods, including large mammals. Grizzlies are also strong swimmers and fast runners.

Predator Facts...

While reticulated pythons are actually longer, green anaconda are far heavier; the females, generally larger than males, can reach 250 kilograms (550 lbs), grow to nine meters (over 29 feet) long and reach 30 centimeters (12 in) in diameter. They are not venomous but instead use their immense muscular power to constrict and suffocate their prey, which includes capybara, deer, caiman, and even jaguars.

Predator Facts...

This animal is known as the "king of the jungle," and for good reason. Lions hunt some of the largest prey on Earth, including buffalo and wildebeest. Part of their terrific success as predators comes from the fact that they cooperate in their kills. Lions live in social groups called prides, and all members work together in the hunt.

Predator Facts...

Orcas are apex predators, with no animals that hunt them (except for humans). They even prey on large whales and sharks. Orcas are sometimes called the wolves of the sea, because they hunt in groups like wolf packs. Killer whales' sophisticated hunting techniques and vocal behaviors, which are often specific to a particular group and passed across generations, have been described as manifestations of culture.

Predator Facts...

The Saltwater Crocodile has been known to eat everything from water buffalo to sharks. In order to kill its food it make use of a technique called the "death roll" where it relentlessly flips its prey over and over in the water until it drowns and then comes apart.

Predator Facts...

Although they are mostly herbivorous, they are also highly aggressive and are widely regarded as one of the most dangerous animals in Africa. They have been known to attack humans without provocation even to the point of destroying entire vehicles.

Predator Facts...

Tigers prefer to hunt large prey by ambush. If you look at a tiger, it is less likely to attack, as it has lost the element of surprise. In some locations in India, people traditionally wear a mask on the back of their head while walking through forests to prevent tigers from pouncing from behind.

Predator Facts...

Very much like Polar Bears, Komodo Dragons are not picky eaters. They will eat anything from birds to water buffalos to humans and they have even been known to dig up bodies from shallow graves. They are prodigious hunters and will wait stealthily until their prey approaches after which they will charge forward, rip out its throat, and retreat while it bleeds out.

Predator Facts...

Wolves live and hunt in packs. They are known to roam large distances, perhaps 20 km in a single day. Wolf packs in the far north often travel hundreds of km each year and this is due to them following migrating herds. Wolves are highly territorial animals, and generally establish territories far larger than they require to survive; in order to assure a steady supply of prey.

Predator Facts...

When most animals are wounded they run away and hide. Not leopards. When these dangerous creatures are wounded they become even more dangerous. Not only that, but they're strong. They are pound for pound the strongest of the big cats. They are able to climb trees, even when carrying heavy prey, and often choose to rest on tree branches during the day. One reason why leopards sometimes take their prey up in the trees is to ensure lions or hyenas can't steal them.

Predator Facts...

The Eastern Diamondback in considered the most venomous species in North America. Surprisingly, juveniles are considered more dangerous than adults, due to their inability to control the amount of venom injected. Most species of rattlesnakes have hemotoxic venom, destroying tissue, degenerating organs and causing coagulopathy (disrupted blood clotting).

Predator Facts...

Black panthers have large and strong paws and sharp claws that are used for hunting. Panther can survive in areas populated with humans better than other cats. It is the fifth largest species of cat as it has a very large skull and long body, but its legs are short. Their large skull makes for a very strong jaw, with which they can even attack and kill a giraffe.

Predator Facts...

A black caiman is basically an alligator on steroids. They can grow up to six meters (20 feet) long, with bigger, heavier skulls than Nile crocodiles, and are the apex predator in the Amazonian waters. That means they are basically the kings of the river—they eat nearly anything they can get their teeth into, including piranhas, monkeys, perch, deer, and anaconda.

Predator Facts...

Bull sharks live in both the fresh water and salt water found around the world. The bull shark is classified as number three on the list of most dangerous sharks in the world when it comes to attacks on humans. They don't move very fast but they are certainly able to tackle their prey due to their sheer strength. They are unpredictable and that is what makes them so dangerous.

Predator Facts...

The praying mantis is so named because when waiting for prey, it holds its front legs in an upright position, as if they are folded in prayer. Don't be fooled by its angelic pose, however, because the mantis is a deadly predator. They even cannibalize their sex partners.

Predator Facts...

Responsible for the majority of snake related deaths in the world, this viper uses a hemotoxin similar to that of the boomslang. Unfortunately most of the bites occur in areas that lack modern medical facilities so the victims slowly bleed to death over the course of several weeks.

Predator Facts...

These legendary predators have a terrible time distinguishing between the edible and the non-edible. There chosen method? Sampling. They sample buoys, boats, surfboards, humans, anything that floats. Contrary to popular belief, however, they really aren't man-eaters. Humans are too bony, and after the initial bite, they usually leave you to bleed out in the water.

Predator Facts...

Eagle owls are among the largest winged hunters on the planet and combine their size with incredible ferocity. They will eat almost anything and stop at nothing. According to one report, a young wolf was attacked, while small deer and even foxes are taken with regularity. In one spectacular attack, a Veraux's eagle owl killed a massive, cobra-eating secretary bird.

Predator Facts...

The Goliath Bird-Eater Spider is actually one that belongs to the Tarantula group. Spider was named early on by explorers. They happened to see one eating a Humming Bird. They have a great deal of hair covering them. They can be very fast and very nervous. You want to avoid touching them too. Their hairs can make your skin very irritated and their fangs are dangerous.

Predator Facts...

Unlike most other animals on this list, the world's largest carnivore is not afraid of you. It has no natural predators and will eat anything that is even slightly meaty, including other polar bears. Although they generally don't kill humans, it's probably because there aren't many of them around to kill.

CPSIA information can be obtained
at www.ICGtesting.com
Printed in the USA
BVHW011254041219
565639BV00012B/105/P